GOODBYE!

THE LAST DAY

OF SCHOOL

WILL BE

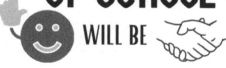

Guest Book To

Celebrate

ADVICE & WISHES FOR THE GRADUATE

Be Prepared To ....

....

Always Keep..

....

Focus On ....

Never ....

Always Remember..

....

Be Open To...

....

Surround Yourself With ....

....

I Wish You..

....

(One Last Thing)...

....

BEST WISHES ....

AUTOGRAPH

ADVICE & WISHES FOR THE GRADUATE

Be Prepared To ....

Always Keep ....

Focus On ....

Never ....

Always Remember ....

Be Open To ....

Surround Yourself With ....

I Wish You ....

(One Last Thing) ....

BEST WISHES ....

AUTOGRAPH

ADVICE & WISHES FOR THE GRADUATE

Be Prepared To ....
....

Always Keep...

....

Focus On ....

Never ....

Always Remember...

....

Be Open To..

....

Surround Yourself With ....

....

I Wish You..

....

(One Last Thing)..

....

BEST WISHES ....

AUTOGRAPH

ADVICE & WISHES FOR THE GRADUATE

Be Prepared To ....
....

Always Keep ....
....

Focus On ....

Never ....

Always Remember ....
....

Be Open To ....
....

Surround Yourself With ....
....

I Wish You ....
....

(One Last Thing) ....
....

BEST WISHES ....

AUTOGRAPH

ADVICE & WISHES FOR THE GRADUATE

Be Prepared To ....
....

Always Keep ....
....

Focus On ....

Never ....

Always Remember ....
....

Be Open To ....
....

Surround Yourself With ....
....

I Wish You ....
....

(One Last Thing) ....
....

BEST WISHES ....

AUTOGRAPH

ADVICE & WISHES FOR THE GRADUATE

Be Prepared To ....

....

Always Keep ....

....

Focus On ....

Never ....

Always Remember ....

....

Be Open To ....

....

Surround Yourself With ....

....

I Wish You ....

....

(One Last Thing) ....

....

BEST WISHES ....

AUTOGRAPH

ADVICE & WISHES FOR THE GRADUATE

Be Prepared To ....

....

Always Keep..

....

Focus On ....

Never ....

Always Remember...

....

Be Open To..

....

Surround Yourself With ....

....

I Wish You..

....

(One Last Thing)...

....

BEST WISHES ....

AUTOGRAPH

ADVICE & WISHES FOR THE GRADUATE

Be Prepared To ....

....

Always Keep ....

....

Focus On ....

Never ....

Always Remember ....

....

Be Open To ....

....

Surround Yourself With ....

....

I Wish You ....

....

(One Last Thing) ....

....

BEST WISHES ....

AUTOGRAPH

ADVICE & WISHES FOR THE GRADUATE

Be Prepared To ....
....

Always Keep ....
....

Focus On ....

Never ....

Always Remember ....
....

Be Open To ....
....

Surround Yourself With ....
....

I Wish You ....
....

(One Last Thing) ....
....

BEST WISHES ....

AUTOGRAPH

ADVICE & WISHES FOR THE GRADUATE

Be Prepared To ....
....

Always Keep ....
....

Focus On ....

Never ....

Always Remember ....
....

Be Open To ....
....

Surround Yourself With ....
....

I Wish You ....
....

(One Last Thing) ....
....

BEST WISHES ....

AUTOGRAPH

ADVICE & WISHES FOR THE GRADUATE

Be Prepared To ....
....

Always Keep..
....

Focus On ....

Never ....

Always Remember...
....

Be Open To..
....

Surround Yourself With ....
....

I Wish You...
....

(One Last Thing)...
....

BEST WISHES ....

AUTOGRAPH

ADVICE & WISHES FOR THE GRADUATE

Be Prepared To ....
....

Always Keep ....
....

Focus On ....

Never ....

Always Remember ....
....

Be Open To ....
....

Surround Yourself With ....
....

I Wish You ....
....

(One Last Thing) ....
....

BEST WISHES ....

AUTOGRAPH

ADVICE & WISHES FOR THE GRADUATE

Be Prepared To ....
....

Always Keep..
....

Focus On ....

Never ....

Always Remember..
....

Be Open To..
....

Surround Yourself With ....
....

I Wish You..
....

(One Last Thing)..
....

BEST WISHES ....

AUTOGRAPH

ADVICE & WISHES FOR THE GRADUATE

Be Prepared To ....

....

Always Keep ....

....

Focus On ....

Never ....

Always Remember ....

....

Be Open To ....

....

Surround Yourself With ....

....

I Wish You ....

....

(One Last Thing) ....

....

BEST WISHES ....

AUTOGRAPH

ADVICE & WISHES FOR THE GRADUATE

Be Prepared To ....
....

Always Keep ....
....

Focus On ....

Never ....

Always Remember ....
....

Be Open To ....
....

Surround Yourself With ....
....

I Wish You ....
....

(One Last Thing) ....
....

BEST WISHES ....

AUTOGRAPH

ADVICE & WISHES FOR THE GRADUATE

Be Prepared To ....
....

Always Keep...

....

Focus On ....

Never ....

Always Remember..

....

Be Open To...

....

Surround Yourself With ....

....

I Wish You..

....

(One Last Thing)..

....

BEST WISHES ....

AUTOGRAPH

ADVICE & WISHES FOR THE GRADUATE

Be Prepared To ....
....

Always Keep ....
....

Focus On ....

Never ....

Always Remember ....
....

Be Open To ....
....

Surround Yourself With ....
....

I Wish You ....
....

(One Last Thing) ....
....

BEST WISHES ....

AUTOGRAPH

ADVICE & WISHES FOR THE GRADUATE

Be Prepared To ....
....

Always Keep..
....

Focus On ....

Never...

Always Remember...
....

Be Open To..
....

Surround Yourself With ....
....

I Wish You...
....

(One Last Thing)...
....

BEST WISHES ....

AUTOGRAPH

ADVICE & WISHES FOR THE GRADUATE

Be Prepared To ....

....

Always Keep ....

....

Focus On ....

Never ....

Always Remember ....

....

Be Open To ....

....

Surround Yourself With ....

....

I Wish You ....

....

(One Last Thing) ....

....

BEST WISHES ....

AUTOGRAPH

ADVICE & WISHES FOR THE GRADUATE

Be Prepared To ....

....

Always Keep ....

....

Focus On ....

Never ....

Always Remember ....

....

Be Open To ....

....

Surround Yourself With ....

....

I Wish You ....

....

(One Last Thing) ....

....

BEST WISHES ....

AUTOGRAPH

ADVICE & WISHES FOR THE GRADUATE

Be Prepared To ....
....

Always Keep ....
....

Focus On ....

Never ....

Always Remember ....
....

Be Open To ....
....

Surround Yourself With ....
....

I Wish You ....
....

(One Last Thing) ....
....

BEST WISHES ....

AUTOGRAPH

ADVICE & WISHES FOR THE GRADUATE

Be Prepared To ....

....

Always Keep...

....

Focus On ....

Never ....

Always Remember...

....

Be Open To...

....

Surround Yourself With ....

....

I Wish You...

....

(One Last Thing)..

....

BEST WISHES ....

AUTOGRAPH

ADVICE & WISHES FOR THE GRADUATE

Be Prepared To ....
....

Always Keep...
....

Focus On ....

Never ....

Always Remember...
....

Be Open To..
....

Surround Yourself With ....
....

I Wish You...
....

(One Last Thing)..
....

BEST WISHES ....

AUTOGRAPH

ADVICE & WISHES FOR THE GRADUATE

Be Prepared To ....

....

Always Keep...

....

Focus On ....

Never ....

Always Remember...

....

Be Open To..

....

Surround Yourself With ....

....

I Wish You..

....

(One Last Thing)...

....

BEST WISHES ....

AUTOGRAPH

ADVICE & WISHES FOR THE GRADUATE

Be Prepared To ....
....

Always Keep ....
....

Focus On ....

Never ....

Always Remember ....
....

Be Open To ....
....

Surround Yourself With ....
....

I Wish You ....
....

(One Last Thing) ....
....

BEST WISHES ....

AUTOGRAPH

ADVICE & WISHES FOR THE GRADUATE

Be Prepared To ....
....

Always Keep ....
....

Focus On ....

Never ....

Always Remember ....
....

Be Open To ....
....

Surround Yourself With ....
....

I Wish You ....
....

(One Last Thing) ....
....

BEST WISHES ....

AUTOGRAPH

ADVICE & WISHES FOR THE GRADUATE

Be Prepared To ....
....

Always Keep ....
....

Focus On ....

Never ....

Always Remember ....
....

Be Open To ....
....

Surround Yourself With ....
....

I Wish You ....
....

(One Last Thing) ....
....

BEST WISHES ....

AUTOGRAPH

ADVICE & WISHES FOR THE GRADUATE

Be Prepared To ....
....

Always Keep...
....

Focus On ....

Never...

Always Remember..
....

Be Open To...
....

Surround Yourself With ....
....

I Wish You..
....

(One Last Thing)..
....

BEST WISHES ....

AUTOGRAPH

ADVICE & WISHES FOR THE GRADUATE

Be Prepared To ....
....

Always Keep...
....

Focus On ....

Never ....

Always Remember...
....

Be Open To...
....

Surround Yourself With ....
....

I Wish You...
....

(One Last Thing)...
....

BEST WISHES ....

AUTOGRAPH

ADVICE & WISHES FOR THE GRADUATE

Be Prepared To ....
....

Always Keep ....
....

Focus On ....

Never ....

Always Remember ....
....

Be Open To ....
....

Surround Yourself With ....
....

I Wish You ....
....

(One Last Thing) ....
....

BEST WISHES ....

AUTOGRAPH

ADVICE & WISHES FOR THE GRADUATE

Be Prepared To ....

....

Always Keep ....

....

Focus On ....

Never ....

Always Remember ....

....

Be Open To ....

....

Surround Yourself With ....

....

I Wish You ....

....

(One Last Thing) ....

....

BEST WISHES ....

AUTOGRAPH

ADVICE & WISHES FOR THE GRADUATE

Be Prepared To ....
....

Always Keep ....

....

Focus On ....

Never ....

Always Remember ....

....

Be Open To ....

....

Surround Yourself With ....

....

I Wish You ....

....

(One Last Thing) ....

....

BEST WISHES ....

AUTOGRAPH

ADVICE & WISHES FOR THE GRADUATE

Be Prepared To ....
....

Always Keep..
....

Focus On ....

Never ....

Always Remember...
....

Be Open To..
....

Surround Yourself With ....
....

I Wish You...
....

(One Last Thing)...
....

BEST WISHES ....

AUTOGRAPH

ADVICE & WISHES FOR THE GRADUATE

Be Prepared To ....
....

Always Keep..
....

Focus On ....

Never ....

Always Remember..
....

Be Open To..
....

Surround Yourself With ....
....

I Wish You..
....

(One Last Thing)..
....

BEST WISHES ....

AUTOGRAPH

ADVICE & WISHES FOR THE GRADUATE

Be Prepared To ....
....

Always Keep..
....

Focus On ....

Never ....

Always Remember..
....

Be Open To..
....

Surround Yourself With ....
....

I Wish You..
....

(One Last Thing)..
....

BEST WISHES ....

AUTOGRAPH

ADVICE & WISHES FOR THE GRADUATE

Be Prepared To ....

....

Always Keep ....

....

Focus On ....

Never ....

Always Remember ....

....

Be Open To ....

....

Surround Yourself With ....

....

I Wish You ....

....

(One Last Thing) ....

....

BEST WISHES ....

AUTOGRAPH

ADVICE & WISHES FOR THE GRADUATE

Be Prepared To ....

Always Keep ....

Focus On ....

Never ....

Always Remember ....

Be Open To ....

Surround Yourself With ....

I Wish You ....

(One Last Thing) ....

BEST WISHES ....

AUTOGRAPH

ADVICE & WISHES FOR THE GRADUATE

Be Prepared To ....
....

Always Keep ....
....

Focus On ....

Never ....

Always Remember ....
....

Be Open To ....
....

Surround Yourself With ....
....

I Wish You ....
....

(One Last Thing) ....
....

BEST WISHES ....

AUTOGRAPH

ADVICE & WISHES FOR THE GRADUATE

Be Prepared To ....
....

Always Keep ....
....

Focus On ....
Never ....
Always Remember ....
....

Be Open To ....
....

Surround Yourself With ....
....

I Wish You ....
....

(One Last Thing) ....
....

BEST WISHES ....

AUTOGRAPH

ADVICE & WISHES FOR THE GRADUATE

Be Prepared To ....
....

Always Keep..
....

Focus On ....

Never ....

Always Remember..
....

Be Open To...
....

Surround Yourself With ....
....

I Wish You...
....

(One Last Thing)...
....

BEST WISHES ....

AUTOGRAPH

ADVICE & WISHES FOR THE GRADUATE

Be Prepared To ....
....

Always Keep...
....

Focus On ....

Never ....

Always Remember...
....

Be Open To...
....

Surround Yourself With ....
....

I Wish You...
....

(One Last Thing)..
....

BEST WISHES ....

AUTOGRAPH

ADVICE & WISHES FOR THE GRADUATE

Be Prepared To ....

....

Always Keep...

....

Focus On ....

Never...

Always Remember...

....

Be Open To...

....

Surround Yourself With ....

....

I Wish You..

....

(One Last Thing)..

....

BEST WISHES ....

AUTOGRAPH

ADVICE & WISHES FOR THE GRADUATE

Be Prepared To ....

....

Always Keep ....

....

Focus On ....

Never ....

Always Remember ....

....

Be Open To ....

....

Surround Yourself With ....

....

I Wish You ....

....

(One Last Thing) ....

....

BEST WISHES ....

AUTOGRAPH

ADVICE & WISHES FOR THE GRADUATE

Be Prepared To ....
....

Always Keep ....
....

Focus On ....

Never ....

Always Remember ....
....

Be Open To ....
....

Surround Yourself With ....
....

I Wish You ....
....

(One Last Thing) ....
....

BEST WISHES ....

AUTOGRAPH

ADVICE & WISHES FOR THE GRADUATE

Be Prepared To ....
....

Always Keep ....

....

Focus On ....

Never ....

Always Remember ....

....

Be Open To ....

....

Surround Yourself With ....

....

I Wish You ....

....

(One Last Thing) ....

....

BEST WISHES ....

AUTOGRAPH

ADVICE & WISHES FOR THE GRADUATE

Be Prepared To ....
....

Always Keep...
....

Focus On ....

Never ....

Always Remember...
....

Be Open To...
....

Surround Yourself With ....
....

I Wish You..
....

(One Last Thing)..
....

BEST WISHES ....

AUTOGRAPH

ADVICE & WISHES FOR THE GRADUATE

Be Prepared To ....
....

Always Keep...
....

Focus On ....

Never ....

Always Remember...
....

Be Open To..
....

Surround Yourself With ....
....

I Wish You..
....

(One Last Thing)..
....

BEST WISHES ....

AUTOGRAPH

ADVICE & WISHES FOR THE GRADUATE

Be Prepared To ....
....

Always Keep ....
....

Focus On ....

Never ....

Always Remember...
....

Be Open To..
....

Surround Yourself With ....
....

I Wish You...
....

(One Last Thing)..
....

BEST WISHES ....

AUTOGRAPH

ADVICE & WISHES FOR THE GRADUATE

Be Prepared To ....
....

Always Keep ....
....

Focus On ....

Never ....

Always Remember ....

Be Open To ....
....

Surround Yourself With ....
....

I Wish You ....
....

(One Last Thing) ....
....

BEST WISHES ....

AUTOGRAPH

ADVICE & WISHES FOR THE GRADUATE

Be Prepared To ....

....

Always Keep..

....

Focus On ....

Never ....

Always Remember...

....

Be Open To...

....

Surround Yourself With ....

....

I Wish You ....

....

(One Last Thing)...

....

BEST WISHES ....

AUTOGRAPH

ADVICE & WISHES FOR THE GRADUATE

Be Prepared To ....
....

Always Keep..
....

Focus On ....

Never ....

Always Remember...
....

Be Open To..
....

Surround Yourself With ....
....

I Wish You...
....

(One Last Thing)...
....

BEST WISHES ....

AUTOGRAPH

ADVICE & WISHES FOR THE GRADUATE

Be Prepared To ....
....

Always Keep ....
....

Focus On ....

Never ....

Always Remember ....
....

Be Open To ....
....

Surround Yourself With ....
....

I Wish You ....
....

(One Last Thing) ....
....

BEST WISHES ....

AUTOGRAPH

ADVICE & WISHES FOR THE GRADUATE

Be Prepared To ....
....

Always Keep ....
....

Focus On ....

Never ....

Always Remember ....
....

Be Open To ....
....

Surround Yourself With ....
....

1 Wish You ....
....

(One Last Thing) ....
....

BEST WISHES ....

AUTOGRAPH

ADVICE & WISHES FOR THE GRADUATE

Be Prepared To ....
....

Always Keep ....
....

Focus On ....

Never ....

Always Remember ....
....

Be Open To ....
....

Surround Yourself With ....
....

I Wish You ....
....

(One Last Thing) ....
....

BEST WISHES ....

AUTOGRAPH

ADVICE & WISHES FOR THE GRADUATE

Be Prepared To ....
....

Always Keep ....
....

Focus On ....

Never ....

Always Remember ....
....

Be Open To ....
....

Surround Yourself With ....
....

I Wish You ....
....

(One Last Thing) ....
....

BEST WISHES ....

AUTOGRAPH

ADVICE & WISHES FOR THE GRADUATE

Be Prepared To ....
....

Always Keep ....
....

Focus On ....

Never ....

Always Remember ....
....

Be Open To ....
....

Surround Yourself With ....
....

I Wish You ....
....

(One Last Thing) ....
....

BEST WISHES ....

AUTOGRAPH

ADVICE & WISHES FOR THE GRADUATE

Be Prepared To ....
....

Always Keep ....
....

Focus On ....

Never ....

Always Remember ....
....

Be Open To ....
....

Surround Yourself With ....
....

I Wish You ....
....

(One Last Thing) ....
....

BEST WISHES ....

AUTOGRAPH

ADVICE & WISHES FOR THE GRADUATE

Be Prepared To ....
....

Always Keep...

....

Focus On ....

Never ....

Always Remember...

....

Be Open To..

....

Surround Yourself With ....

....

I Wish You...

....

(One Last Thing)...

....

BEST WISHES ....

AUTOGRAPH

ADVICE & WISHES FOR THE GRADUATE

Be Prepared To ....
....

Always Keep ....
....

Focus On ....

Never ....

Always Remember ....
....

Be Open To ....
....

Surround Yourself With ....
....

I Wish You ....
....

(One Last Thing) ....
....

BEST WISHES ....

AUTOGRAPH

ADVICE & WISHES FOR THE GRADUATE

Be Prepared To ....

....

Always Keep...

....

Focus On ....

Never...

Always Remember..

....

Be Open To..

....

Surround Yourself With ....

....

I Wish You..

....

(One Last Thing)..

....

BEST WISHES ....

AUTOGRAPH

ADVICE & WISHES FOR THE GRADUATE

Be Prepared To ....
....

Always Keep ....

....

Focus On ....

Never ....

Always Remember ....

....

Be Open To ....

....

Surround Yourself With ....

....

I Wish You ....

....

(One Last Thing) ....

....

BEST WISHES ....

AUTOGRAPH

ADVICE & WISHES FOR THE GRADUATE

Be Prepared To ....

....

Always Keep...

....

Focus On ....

Never..

Always Remember...

....

Be Open To...

....

Surround Yourself With ....

....

I Wish You..

....

(One Last Thing)...

....

BEST WISHES ....

AUTOGRAPH

ADVICE & WISHES FOR THE GRADUATE

Be Prepared To ....

Always Keep ....

Focus On ....

Never ....

Always Remember ....

Be Open To ....

Surround Yourself With ....

I Wish You ....

(One Last Thing) ....

BEST WISHES ....

AUTOGRAPH

ADVICE & WISHES FOR THE GRADUATE

Be Prepared To ....
....

Always Keep ....
....

Focus On ....

Never ....

Always Remember ....
....

Be Open To ....
....

Surround Yourself With ....
....

I Wish You ....
....

(One Last Thing) ....
....

BEST WISHES ....

AUTOGRAPH

ADVICE & WISHES FOR THE GRADUATE

Be Prepared To ....
....

Always Keep ....
....

Focus On ....

Never ....

Always Remember ....
....

Be Open To ....
....

Surround Yourself With ....
....

I Wish You ....
....

(One Last Thing) ....
....

BEST WISHES ....

AUTOGRAPH

ADVICE & WISHES FOR THE GRADUATE

Be Prepared To ....
....

Always Keep ....

....

Focus On ....

Never ....

Always Remember ....

....

Be Open To ....

....

Surround Yourself With ....

....

I Wish You ....

....

(One Last Thing) ....

....

BEST WISHES ....

AUTOGRAPH

ADVICE & WISHES FOR THE GRADUATE

Be Prepared To ....

Always Keep ....

Focus On ....

Never ....

Always Remember ....

Be Open To ....

Surround Yourself With ....

I Wish You ....

(One Last Thing) ....

BEST WISHES ....

AUTOGRAPH

ADVICE & WISHES FOR THE GRADUATE

Be Prepared To ....
....

Always Keep...
....

Focus On ....

Never..

Always Remember...
....

Be Open To...
....

Surround Yourself With ....
....

I Wish You..
....

(One Last Thing)..
....

BEST WISHES ....

AUTOGRAPH

ADVICE & WISHES FOR THE GRADUATE

Be Prepared To ....

....

Always Keep ....

....

Focus On ....

Never ....

Always Remember ....

....

Be Open To ....

....

Surround Yourself With ....

....

I Wish You ....

....

(One Last Thing) ....

....

BEST WISHES ....

AUTOGRAPH

ADVICE & WISHES FOR THE GRADUATE

Be Prepared To ....
....

Always Keep...
....

Focus On ....

Never ....

Always Remember...
....

Be Open To...
....

Surround Yourself With ....
....

I Wish You···

(One Last Thing)···
···

BEST WISHES ···

AUTOGRAPH

ADVICE & WISHES FOR THE GRADUATE

Be Prepared To ....
....

Always Keep ....

....

Focus On ....

Never ....

Always Remember ....

....

Be Open To ....

....

Surround Yourself With ....

....

I Wish You ....

....

(One Last Thing) ....

....

BEST WISHES ....

AUTOGRAPH

ADVICE & WISHES FOR THE GRADUATE

Be Prepared To ....
....

Always Keep ....
....

Focus On ....

Never ....

Always Remember ....
....

Be Open To ....
....

Surround Yourself With ....
....

I Wish You ....
....

(One Last Thing) ....
....

BEST WISHES ....

AUTOGRAPH

ADVICE & WISHES FOR THE GRADUATE

Be Prepared To ....
....

Always Keep...
....

Focus On ....

Never ....

Always Remember...
....

Be Open To...
....

Surround Yourself With ....
....

I Wish You..
....

(One Last Thing)..
....

BEST WISHES ....

AUTOGRAPH

ADVICE & WISHES FOR THE GRADUATE

Be Prepared To ....
....

Always Keep...
....

Focus On ....

Never ....

Always Remember...
....

Be Open To...
....

Surround Yourself With ....
....

I Wish You..
....

(One Last Thing)...
....

BEST WISHES ....

AUTOGRAPH

ADVICE & WISHES FOR THE GRADUATE

Be Prepared To ....
....

Always Keep ....
....

Focus On ....

Never ....

Always Remember ....
....

Be Open To ....
....

Surround Yourself With ....
....

I Wish You ....
....

(One Last Thing) ....
....

BEST WISHES ....

AUTOGRAPH

ADVICE & WISHES FOR THE GRADUATE

Be Prepared To ....

....

Always Keep ....

....

Focus On ....

Never ....

Always Remember ....

....

Be Open To ....

....

Surround Yourself With ....

....

I Wish You ....

....

(One Last Thing) ....

....

BEST WISHES ....

AUTOGRAPH

ADVICE & WISHES FOR THE GRADUATE

Be Prepared To ....
....

Always Keep ....

....

Focus On ....

Never ....

Always Remember ....

....

Be Open To ....

....

Surround Yourself With ....

....

I Wish You ....

....

(One Last Thing) ....

....

BEST WISHES ....

AUTOGRAPH

ADVICE & WISHES FOR THE GRADUATE

Be Prepared To ....
....

Always Keep ....

....

Focus On ....

Never ....

Always Remember ....
....

Be Open To ....
....

Surround Yourself With ....
....

I Wish You ....
....

(One Last Thing) ....
....

BEST WISHES ....

AUTOGRAPH

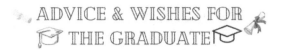

ADVICE & WISHES FOR THE GRADUATE

Be Prepared To ....
....

Always Keep...
....

Focus On ....

Never ....

Always Remember..
....

Be Open To...
....

Surround Yourself With ....
....

I Wish You...
....

(One Last Thing)...
....

BEST WISHES ....

AUTOGRAPH

ADVICE & WISHES FOR THE GRADUATE

Be Prepared To ....
....

Always Keep...
....

Focus On ....

Never...

Always Remember...
....

Be Open To...
....

Surround Yourself With ....
....

I Wish You...
....

(One Last Thing)...
....

BEST WISHES ....

AUTOGRAPH

ADVICE & WISHES FOR THE GRADUATE

Be Prepared To ....
....

Always Keep ....
....

Focus On ....

Never ....

Always Remember ....
....

Be Open To ....
....

Surround Yourself With ....
....

I Wish You ....
....

(One Last Thing) ....
....

BEST WISHES ....

AUTOGRAPH

ADVICE & WISHES FOR THE GRADUATE

Be Prepared To ....
....

Always Keep ....
....

Focus On ....

Never ....

Always Remember..
....

Be Open To..
....

Surround Yourself With ....
....

I Wish You...
....

(One Last Thing)...
....

BEST WISHES ....

AUTOGRAPH

ADVICE & WISHES FOR THE GRADUATE

Be Prepared To ....
....

Always Keep ....
....

Focus On ....

Never ....

Always Remember ....
....

Be Open To ....
....

Surround Yourself With ....
....

I Wish You ....
....

(One Last Thing) ....
....

BEST WISHES ....

AUTOGRAPH

ADVICE & WISHES FOR THE GRADUATE

Be Prepared To ....
....

Always Keep..
....

Focus On ....

Never..

Always Remember..
....

Be Open To..
....

Surround Yourself With ....
....

I Wish You...
....

(One Last Thing)..
....

BEST WISHES ....

AUTOGRAPH

ADVICE & WISHES FOR THE GRADUATE

Be Prepared To ....
....

Always Keep ....
....

Focus On ....

Never ....

Always Remember ....
....

Be Open To ....
....

Surround Yourself With ....
....

1 Wish You ....
....

(One Last Thing) ....
....

BEST WISHES ....

AUTOGRAPH

ADVICE & WISHES FOR THE GRADUATE

Be Prepared To ....
....

Always Keep...
....

Focus On ....

Never ....

Always Remember...
....

Be Open To..
....

Surround Yourself With ....
....

I Wish You...
....

(One Last Thing)..
....

BEST WISHES ....

AUTOGRAPH

ADVICE & WISHES FOR THE GRADUATE

Be Prepared To ....
....

Always Keep ....
....

Focus On ....

Never ....

Always Remember ....
....

Be Open To ....
....

Surround Yourself With ....
....

I Wish You ....
....

(One Last Thing) ....
....

BEST WISHES ....

AUTOGRAPH

ADVICE & WISHES FOR THE GRADUATE

Be Prepared To ....

....

Always Keep..

....

Focus On ....

Never..

Always Remember..

....

Be Open To..

....

Surround Yourself With ....

....

I Wish You..

....

(One Last Thing)..

....

BEST WISHES ....

AUTOGRAPH

ADVICE & WISHES FOR THE GRADUATE

Be Prepared To ....
....

Always Keep...
....

Focus On ....

Never ....

Always Remember..
....

Be Open To...
....

Surround Yourself With ....
....

I Wish You..
....

(One Last Thing)..
....

BEST WISHES ....

AUTOGRAPH

ADVICE & WISHES FOR THE GRADUATE

Be Prepared To ....

Always Keep ....

Focus On ....

Never ....

Always Remember ....

Be Open To ....

Surround Yourself With ....

I Wish You ....

(One Last Thing) ....

BEST WISHES ....

AUTOGRAPH

ADVICE & WISHES FOR THE GRADUATE

Be Prepared To ....

....

Always Keep...

....

Focus On ....

Never ....

Always Remember...

....

Be Open To...

....

Surround Yourself With ....

....

I Wish You...

....

(One Last Thing)...

....

BEST WISHES ....

AUTOGRAPH

ADVICE & WISHES FOR THE GRADUATE

Be Prepared To ....
....

Always Keep..
....

Focus On ....

Never...

Always Remember...
....

Be Open To...
....

Surround Yourself With ....
....

I Wish You...
....

(One Last Thing)...
....

BEST WISHES ....

AUTOGRAPH

ADVICE & WISHES FOR THE GRADUATE

Be Prepared To ....
....

Always Keep ....
....

Focus On ....

Never ....

Always Remember ....
....

Be Open To ....
....

Surround Yourself With ....
....

I Wish You ....
....

(One Last Thing) ....
....

BEST WISHES ....

AUTOGRAPH

ADVICE & WISHES FOR THE GRADUATE

Be Prepared To ....
....

Always Keep...

....

Focus On ....

Never ....

Always Remember...

....

Be Open To...

....

Surround Yourself With ....

....

I Wish You ....

....

(One Last Thing)..

....

BEST WISHES ....

AUTOGRAPH

ADVICE & WISHES FOR THE GRADUATE

Be Prepared To ....
....

Always Keep...

....

Focus On ....

Never ....

Always Remember...
....

Be Open To...

....

Surround Yourself With ....

....

I Wish You...

....

(One Last Thing)...

....

BEST WISHES ....

AUTOGRAPH

ADVICE & WISHES FOR THE GRADUATE

Be Prepared To ....
....

Always Keep..
....

Focus On ....

Never..

Always Remember...
....

Be Open To..
....

Surround Yourself With ....
....

I Wish You..
....

(One Last Thing)..
....

BEST WISHES ....

AUTOGRAPH

ADVICE & WISHES FOR THE GRADUATE

Be Prepared To ....
....

Always Keep...
....

Focus On ....

Never ....

Always Remember...
....

Be Open To...
....

Surround Yourself With ....
....

I Wish You...
....

(One Last Thing)...
....

BEST WISHES ....

AUTOGRAPH

ADVICE & WISHES FOR THE GRADUATE

Be Prepared To ....
....

Always Keep ....
....

Focus On ....

Never ....

Always Remember ....
....

Be Open To ....
....

Surround Yourself With ....
....

I Wish You ....
....

(One Last Thing) ....
....

BEST WISHES ....

AUTOGRAPH

ADVICE & WISHES FOR THE GRADUATE

Be Prepared To ....
....

Always Keep ....

....

Focus On ....

Never ....

Always Remember ....

....

Be Open To ....

....

Surround Yourself With ....

....

I Wish You ....

....

(One Last Thing) ....

....

BEST WISHES ....

AUTOGRAPH

Made in United States
North Haven, CT
05 May 2022

18931314R00055